LETTING LOVE GO, LETTING LOVE IN

ASA RAY HENSON

FIRST PRINTING: 2019 ISBN 978-1-79484-334-9

FORWARD ALL INQUIRIES TO THE FOLLOWING:
ASARAYWRITES@GMAIL.COM
ASA RAY HENSON
P.O. BOX 81
ROYSTON, GA 30662

OTHER BOOKS BY ASA RAY HENSON

UNSETTLED & UNSAID

GHOST LETTERS

DEAR RAXLEY

WRITER'S BLOCK

LOVING DAISIES

RED

PROMPT ME TO PROMPT YOU

ROYAL OVERDOSE

SURVIVING 24

FROM THE OUTSIDE LOOKING IN

A HEALING HEART

WE HAVE NO CONTROL OVER WHO OUR HEART DECIDES TO LATCH ON AND CLING TO. THE ONLY PERSON WE CAN MAKE SURE WE LOVE IS OURSELVES. FIND THE TINIEST GLIMMER OF HOPE IN YOURSELF AND LEARN TO LET GO OF THE LOVE THAT HARMS YOU. NOT ALL LOVE IS HEALTHY, BUT YOU DESERVE TO FEEL THE LOVE YOU HAVE FOR YOURSELF AT LEAST ONE DAY. MAKE SURE YOU FEEL SOMETHING REAL.

TELL YOUR FRIENDS YOU LOVE THEM. TELL THEM YOU CARE WHEN THEY DON'T THINK YOU DO. TELL THEM AFTER A LONG EXHAUSTED FIGHT. DON'T WALK AWAY WITHOUT TELLING THEM YOU LOVE THEM. PEOPLE AREN'T MEANT TO LAST FOREVER, BUT IF THEY KNOW YOU LOVE THEM WHEN THEY GO, IT'LL MAKE THINGS EASIER. SWALLOW YOUR PRIDE AND TELL THEM THEY MATTER.

WE HAVEN'T SPOKEN IN FIVE YEARS.

I DON'T CALL YOU TO TELL YOU ABOUT THE GIRL THAT'S STOLEN MY HEART

YOU DON'T HEAR FROM ME WHEN SHE BREAKS IT

THERE'S NO CONTACT OR COMMUNICATION THAT ALLOWS YOU TO SEE INTO

MY LIFE

WHERE I'M AT

WHERE I WORK

WHAT I SPEND MY DAYS DOING

YOU DON'T KNOW WHERE I LIVE

YOU HAVE NO IDEA OF THE PROCESS OF RECOVERING I GO THROUGH

YOU NO LONGER KNOW ME

WE HAVEN'T TALKED IN FIVE YEARS

I HATE TO SAY I'M OKAY WITH THAT

I HATE THAT I AM INDIFFERENT ON WHETHER YOU'RE STILL ALIVE OR NOT

SOME DAYS I WISH YOUR ADDICTION WOULD GO AHEAD AND GET

THE BEST OF YOU

MAYBE THAT'S WRONG OF ME

BUT I WOULD RATHER YOU BE GONE THAN FACING THAT STATE

I'D RATHER YOU NOT BE FACING YOUR DAYS ALONE

WHAT'S A LIFE THAT YOU CAN'T EVEN REMEMBER

I'M SORRY WE DON'T TALK

I'M SORRY I WON'T ATTEND YOUR FUNERAL

I LOVE YOU, BUT YOU LOVED YOUR ADDICTIONS MORE.

SHE IS QUIET IN MY PRESENCE. HER THOUGHTS HAVE SWARMED HER LIKE FLIES, AND SHE DOESN'T HAVE THE VOICE TO SPIT WORDS OUT WELL ENOUGH TO TELL ME WHAT SHE FEELS. SO SHE'S SILENT. THE ONLY SOUNDS BETWEEN US ARE BREATHING AND THE WAY SHE SCRAPES HER HANDS OVER HER EYES TO WIPE AWAY TEARS, AS IF I'LL MAGICALLY BE BLIND IN SEEING THEM. EVEN IN HER SILENCE SHE IS BEAUTIFUL. EVEN IN HER QUIET, SHE LOVES ME MORE FOR EXISTING THERE WITH HER. SOMETIMES YOU DON'T HAVE TO FIX A PROBLEM WITH WORDS OR PHYSICAL REPAIRS. YOU CAN FIX EVERYTHING BY SIMPLY BEING THERE.

LOVE ME HARD BEFORE YOU GO

LOVE ME SOFT DURING YOUR MORNING HELLO

KISS ME SWEET TO START YOUR DAY

KISS ME GENTLE WITH ANY WORDS YOU SAY

STAY WITH ME WHEN THE NIGHTS ARE LONG

RETURN TO ME AFTER BEING GONE TOO LONG

HOLD MY HAND WHEN YOU FEEL PROUD

HOLD ME CLOSE WHEN NOBODY'S AROUND

TOGETHER WE CAN DO GREAT THINGS

TOGETHER OUR GROWTH CAN CONSTANTLY CHANGE

IT'S WEIRD TO ME HOW LIFE CAN BE CHANGED SO MUCH BY MONEY. YOU CAN BE HAPPY WHEN YOU'RE POOR JUST AS MUCH AS YOU CAN BE HAPPY WHEN YOU'RE RICH. YOU FIND JOY IN THE JOB THAT LIGHTS YOUR SPARK INSIDE. I LOVE THAT. AS MUCH AS MONEY CAN CHANGE THE WORLD, YOU CAN CHANGE YOUR AFFECTION FOR IT JUST AS EASILY. IT IS BOTH SOMETHING OF GREAT IMPORTANCE AND SOMETHING THAT HOLDS NO VALUE. PERSPECTIVE IS EVERYTHING.

OBSESS OVER YOURSELF
WAKE IN THE MORNINGS AND SAY HELLO IN PASSING TO THE MIRROR
MAKE YOUR WORLD ABOUT YOU BEFORE MAKING IT ABOUT EVERYONE ELSE
YOU ARE A TREASURE

VOICES SURROUND ME,
COAXING ME INTO A BELIEF OF BEING A FAILURE
NO MATTER HOW FAR I RUN
WHERE I CHOOSE TO HIDE
THEY FIND ME
THEY SCREAM AND LAUGH
TELLING ME HOW I WILL NEVER LIVE UP TO MY OWN STANDARDS
SO WHY TRY TO LIVE UP TO THOSE OF MY LOVED ONES
MY DREAMS? THEY'RE A JOKE TO THE VOICES
BUT I REFUSE TO BELIEVE THEM
I WILL KEEP CHASING
CONTINUE RUNNING FOR THE HILLS AND SPREADING MY WRITING
I WILL SHOUT MY OWN WORDS FROM ROOFTOPS AS PAPER COPIES
SPRINKLE THE GROUND BELOW AND LITTER THE HANDS OF PEOPLE
I AM CAPABLE OF MORE THAN A VOICE TELLING ME I CAN'T

LEARN TO FIND COMFORT IN YOURSELF

PEOPLE IN THIS WORLD WILL BE HARSH

THEY WILL JUDGE YOU FOR WHO YOU MAKE EYE CONTACT WITH

JUST AS MUCH AS THE PERSON YOU KISS

AIM FOR SOMEBODY THAT TREATS YOU WELL, BUT ALSO WHO YOU

WISH TO BE WITH

WHETHER YOU ARE A GIRL DATING A GIRL

A BOY DATING A GIRL

OR ANYONE FALLING IN LOVE WITH ANYONE

YOUR HEART BELONGS TO YOU

IT MAY LOVE SOMEBODY, BUT IT WILL ALWAYS BE YOURS FIRST

LOVE IS LOVE

I AM SORRY IT'S UNSAFE TO ALWAYS LOVE WHO YOU LOVE, BUT I HOPE YOU

CAN FIND THE SAFETY TO DO SO

EVEN IF IT MEANS WALKING AWAY FROM FAMILY

THERE'S SOMETHING ABOUT A PIANO THAT SEEMS LIKE A KEY TO MY SOUL

I FEEL SO MUCH PEACE WHEN IT'S PLAYED

THE KEYS ARE STEPPING STONES THAT SHOW NOTES OF WHO I AM LIKE THEY'RE

PLASTERED ON MY BEDROOM WALL

I HOPE WHEN PEOPLE LISTEN TO A PIANO WITH ME, THEY SEE WHO I AM

I HOPE THEY LOVE WHO I AM

I HOPE THEY FIND ME AS MUCH AS I HAVE FOUND MYSELF

I WANT TO SEE THE WORLD. TO DOCUMENT IT AND SHARE THE BEAUTY OUT THERE WITH EVERYONE I KNOW. I WANT TO DANCE IN THE STREET OF A FOREIGN COUNTRY, LAUGHING AND BONDING REGARDLESS OF ANY LANGUAGE BARRIER. TO SHAKE HANDS AND SHARE FOOD WITH A STRANGER THAT HAS LIVED A LIFE I KNOW NOTHING OF, AND TO LEARN ABOUT THAT LIFE. I WANT TO EXPLORE, SEE WHAT'S OUT THERE AND CONSTANTLY FEEL AMAZED AT HOW MUCH WE MISS OUT ON SEEING. I WANT TO GROW FROM SEEING THE UNIVERSE.

I HOPE YOU FIND THINGS IN LIFE THAT MAKE YOUR HEART LEAP FOR JOY. I HOPE THOSE THINGS WRAP THEIR ARMS AROUND YOU AND HOLD YOU TIGHT WHEN YOU MOST NEED IT. THAT THEY INSPIRE YOU TO BE A BETTER YOU, A HEALTHY YOU. I HOPE THE GOODNESS IN THIS WORLD IS ALWAYS WAITING FOR YOU AROUND EACH CORNER, AND THE LIFE LESSONS YOU LEARN MAKE YOU FEEL STRONGER. YOU ARE DESERVING OF A LIFE FILLED WITH HAPPINESS. A LIFE THAT MAKES YOU REACH FOR MORE. I AM SO GLAD YOU EXIST.

DO YOU EVER LOOK BACK AT WHAT WE SHARED AND WISH YOU'D MADE DIFFERENT CHOICES? THAT YOU'D BEEN MORE HONEST AND GIVEN ME MORE OF A CHANCE INSTEAD OF RUNNING THE SECOND YOU WERE HAPPY? I NO LONGER WISH TO BE WITH YOU, SOMEBODY THAT COULD BREAK MY HEART OR LIE SO EASILY, BUT SOMETIMES I THINK ABOUT IF YOU REGRET IT. I DON'T WANT YOU TO REGRET NOT ENDING UP WITH ME. FOR WHATEVER REASON, WE WEREN'T MEANT TO BE IN THIS LIFETIME. THE UNIVERSE HAD OTHER PLANS.

KISS THE STRANGER
LAUGH WITH THE PEOPLE SEATED NEXT TO YOU
TAKE THE TIME TO HOLD THE DOOR OPEN FOR SOMEBODY
DO THE THINGS THAT SEEM SMALL
OUT OF YOUR COMFORT ZONE

I REMEMBER YOUR MOM SEEING US KISS AND KICKING ME OUT

YOUR TEARS WERE STAINS AT THE TIME

THEY WERE A MIX OF DISAPPOINTMENT AND ANGER

WHILE I FELT OKAY, KNOWING I COULD ALWAYS BE WHO I AM

WITHOUT THE JUDGEMENT OF MY FAMILY

OR AT LEAST WITHOUT HAVING TO BATTLE THEM TO BE MYSELF ANYMORE

YOU STILL HAD TO FIGHT TO BE YOU

I'M SORRY I DIDN'T HAVE THE WORDS TO FIX THINGS THAT NIGHT

I'M SORRY I COULDN'T KISS YOU EVEN MORE IN FRONT OF HER

THAT YOU COULDN'T LOVE ME OPENLY

HOLD YOURSELF TOGETHER

NO MATTER HOW HARD THINGS GET

PICK UP THE PIECES AND KEEP MOVING

YOU WILL FACE CHALLENGE AFTER CHALLENGE

AND YOU WILL OVERCOME ANYTHING YOU PUSH YOURSELF TO KEEP TRYING

YOUR STRENGTH IS SOMETHING THAT MAKES YOU DESERVING OF BEING

IN THE HALL OF FAME

NEVER FORGET YOU HAVE THE ABILITY TO PUT YOURSELF BACK TOGETHER

THERE ARE NIGHTS I DON'T REMEMBER ALMOST AS MUCH AS NIGHTS I DO

FOR THOSE FORGOTTEN MOMENTS, I AM SAD

KNOWING I WAS IN PAIN ENOUGH TO FIND A WAY TO DELETE

BITS OF MY LIFE, MY HEART ACHES

THINKING I COULD BE SO DISTRAUGHT I WOULDN'T WANT TO REMEMBER

I FEEL PITY

GOING FORWARD IN LIFE, I ONLY WISH TO REMEMBER

NO MATTER HOW BAD THE PAIN GETS, I HOPE IT NEVER FINDS ME

HITTING THE DELETE BUTTON

THE LAST DAY WE SPENT TOGETHER YOU COULDN'T LOOK ME IN THE EYES

I TOLD YOU I WAS LEAVING AND YOU CRIED SO HARD I THINK IT BROKE MY

HEART AS MUCH AS IT BROKE YOURS

BUT YOU WOULDN'T LOOK AT ME

YOUR EYES FOUND THE GROUND

THE SKY AS WE WALKED

EVERYWHERE

EVEN AS WE KISSED GOODBYE

I KNEW IT WASN'T A SEE YOU LATER MOMENT

BUT WE BOTH LIED AND SAID WE'D MEET AGAIN

THE FUTURE IS OUT OF OUR CONTROL

YET WE TRY TO CONTROL IT

WE COMMIT TO THINGS WE CAN'T MAKE

WE PROMISE THINGS WE WON'T KEEP

AND THEN WE ONLY ADMIT OUR LACK OF CONTROL WHEN WE CAN USE

IT AS AN EXCUSE

WHY CAN'T WE LIVE OUR LIVES KNOWING WE HAVE ABSOLUTELY NO CONTROL

WHY CAN'T WE LOVE ACCEPTING THE RISK OF IT NOT WORKING OUT

GIVE OUR ALL AND JUST LET GO

I PICKED UP THE PIECES OF MYSELF OFF OF THE SHELVES IN MY ROOM

THE BACKSEAT OF A CAR AS I CRIED

EVERY MISTAKE, MISFORTUNE, OVERTURNED MOMENT

I PICKED UP THE PIECES OF WHO I WAS AND CARRIED

THEM LIKE SHARDS OF GLASS

SOME DAYS I'M NOT SURE HOW I DID IT

HOW I SURVIVED

THE CUTS AND SCARS, THE WOUNDS SO DEEP I COULDN'T SEE,

I HAVE CARRIED THEM WITH ME EVERYWHERE

I WILL ALWAYS CARRY THEM WITH ME

ALL THE WAY TO MY COFFIN

YOU DECIDED TO LOVE SOMEBODY ELSE AND I SAID OKAY. I ACCEPTED THAT FATE WHILE REMAINING BY YOUR SIDE, PLAYING THE ROLE OF A SUPPORTIVE FRIEND. I PUSHED MY FRIENDS ASIDE TO PUT YOUR HAPPINESS FIRST. EVEN WHEN YOU DIDN'T DESERVE IT. THROUGH CHEATING, LIES, MANIPULATION - I WENT WITH IT ALL AS IF IT WERE FINE. I THINK THAT SPEAKS TO MY MENTAL HEALTH FROM BEING WITH YOU MORE THAN I'LL EVER BEGIN TO BE ABLE TO EXPLAIN. I ACCEPTED SO MANY WRONG DOINGS FROM YOU SOLELY SO I DIDN'T HAVE TO FACE MY OWN DEMONS.

IF THERE WERE ONE NIGHT I COULD TRAVEL IN TIME TO, I'D GO BACK TO THE NIGHT WE CAUGHT YOUR JEEP ON FIRE. WE WERE SO CALM ABOUT IT, LAUGHING LIKE HELL LATER ON. AS FLAMES WENT UP AND YOU JUMPED TO PULL US OVER AND PUT THEM OUT WHILE YOU LET ME DRINK MY FEELINGS AWAY. I WOULD GO BACK TO THAT NIGHT OVER ANY OTHER MOMENT IN MY LIFE. JUST TO BE WALKING AROUND WITH YOU ON A COLD ASS MOUNTAIN IN THE PITCH BLACK AGAIN. TO MAKE STUPID JOKES AND ROLL MY EYES WHEN YOU SAID SOMETHING I DIDN'T AGREE WITH. I'D GO BACK TO PUSH YOU IN THE LAKE WITH YOUR CLOTHES ON AND RUIN YOUR BELT. TO RIDE AROUND 'FISHING' ALL NIGHT WHILE WE SAT DRINKING BEER AND PRETENDING WE KNEW WHAT THE HELL WE WERE DOING IN LIFE. IF THERE'S ONE PERSON I'D WANT TO SEE AGAIN, IT'S YOU. THIS LIFE WAS MADE TO HAVE A FRIENDSHIP LIKE YOURS. I AM SO GLAD I HAD ALL THE MOMENTS WITH YOU I DID.
I MISS YOU LIKE CRAZY, FRIEND.

LET GO OF THE HATE IN YOUR HEART

TOSS IT OUT LIKE TRASH FROM YESTERDAY

YOU WILL SPEND MORE TIME ACHING OVER A FEELING THAT DOESN'T DESERVE

YOUR TIME THAN ACTUALLY VALIDATING THE REASON FOR IT

GIVE IT UP LIKE A BAD ADDICTION AND EMBRACE A NEW FEELING

WHENEVER YOU GET THE CHANCE, GET RID OF THE BAD, THE UGLY

YOU ARE FILLED WITH THE BEAUTY OF PORCELAIN

DON'T GIVE UP THE GREATNESS WITHIN OVER PETTY

IN MY MIND YOU ARE STANDING IN FRONT OF ME

A SMILE LIGHTING YOUR FACE FROM EAR TO EAR

DRESSED IN A T-SHIRT AND JEANS, CONTENT

YOUR HANDS ARE GRASPING A CAMERA THAT YOU'VE POINTED AT ME

AND I'M SO WRAPPED UP IN HOW DAMN GORGEOUS YOU LOOK I CAN'T

FOCUS ON ANYTHING SPILLING FROM YOUR LIPS

I KNOW I'M LAUGHING, WATCHING YOU IN AWE

AMAZED AT HOW I'VE NEVER SEEN ANYTHING QUITE LIKE YOU

THE MOON WHISPERS TO ME AT NIGHT,

TELLING ME THE SECRETS OF LIFE AND OF YOU

PROMISING ME IT'LL WORK OUT EVEN WHEN I DON'T EXPECT IT TO

SO I STAY UP LATE LISTENING

LOSING SLEEP IN EXCHANGE FOR THE PEACEFULNESS OF THE MOMENT

TALKING TO THE MOON

WRITERS COME IN A BAKERS DOZEN

ALL WITH THEIR OWN STORY TO TELL

THEIR OWN JOURNEY TO DOCUMENT

MOST PEOPLE FEAR THE COMPETITION

THEY DON'T DEEM EVERYONE ELSE A 'REAL' WRITER

BUT I WANT TO READ THEIR WORDS

I WANT TO UNDERSTAND THEIR STORY

THERE IS MORE TO GRASP THAN THE THOUGHTS I HAVE

I AM NOT THE SPOTLIGHT

I AM NOT THE ONLY ONE WITH GROUNDBREAKING INK TO SPILL

I AM SO GLAD WE CAN SHARE AND THAT I HAVE THAT ABILITY

WE WERE YOUNG ONCE. FIGHTING OVER IRRELEVANT THINGS JUST TO
ENTERTAIN EACH OTHER. BICKERING SO THAT WE KNEW THE OTHER WAS STILL THERE.
WE DROVE EACH OTHER CRAZY. AFTER ALL THESE YEARS, WATCHING EACH OTHER
GROW, I AM AMAZED THAT I STILL LOVE YOU THE SAME. AS MUCH AS I HAVE
ALWAYS RELIED ON YOU IN MY LIFE, I THINK THAT LOVE HAS GROWN IN WAYS.
EVOLVED. NO MATTER THE DISTANCE, THE DAYS WITHOUT TALKING, THE MOMENTS
WE DON'T SHARE. YOU ARE STILL MY HAVEN WHEN LIFE MAKES ME TREMBLE, AND I
AM SO GLAD YOU STILL FEEL YOU CAN CALL ME FROM TIME TO TIME.
FOREVER,
YOUR LOST TREASURE

I USED TO BELIEVE WE'D SIT IN THE MORNINGS SIPPING COFFEE AND STANDING AT THE KITCHEN COUNTER, SO FOCUSED ON EACH OTHER WE'D BE LATE FOR WHATEVER STOOD IN FRONT OF US FOR THE DAY. NOW I SIMPLY LOOK FORWARD TO PASSING YOU IN THE HALLWAY AND SHARING SILENT LOOKS. I LOOK FOR THE MINISCULE TRIVIAL THINGS WITH YOU. THE OPPORTUNITIES TO EXIST ON OUR OWN ONLY TO FIND OUR WAY HOME AND WRAP UP BENEATH THE SAME SHEETS. I DON'T NEED A COZY MORNING KEEPING US FROM OUR BUSY DAYS EVERY SINGLE DAY. I ONLY NEED YOU COMING HOME TO ME AT NIGHT, EXHAUSTED FROM YOUR ADVENTURES AND READY TO CURL IN ON ME AND START A NEW ONE.

DO YOU STILL LOVE AS HARD AS YOU ONCE DID, DARLING?

DO YOU STILL BELIEVE IN YOURSELF LIKE NOTHING HAD

EVER KNOCKED YOU DOWN?

FIND YOURSELF IN EVERYTHING YOU DO

IN THE BOOKS YOU READ

THE MOVIES YOU WATCH

LYRICS YOU SING

FIND YOURSELF IN THE WORK OF OTHERS

THE WORK YOU PUT OUT

YOU ARE MEANT TO BE SEEN

TO BE DISCOVERED

BELIEVE IN EVERYTHING YOU DO

TAKE THE RAGE, THE HAPPY, AND PUT IT INTO THE WORLD IN A WAY

THAT DISPLAYS WHO YOU ARE

FIND YOU EVERY SINGLE DAY

LIKE A GAME OF HIDE AND SEEK

YOU ARE MEANT TO FOUND

I ORIGINALLY HAD ENDED THIS BOOK SUPER SHORT, BUT IF YOU FOUND THIS MEMO BACK HERE THEN I HOPE IT RESONATES WITH YOU.

YOU HAVE SO MUCH POTENTIAL. PLEASE NEVER FORGET THAT. IF YOU DO, HUNT IT DOWN UNTIL YOU BELIEVE IN YOURSELF AGAIN. ALL OF YOUR PAIN, YOUR BATTLE SCARS, YOUR TEARS OF LAUGHTER - THEY ARE MEANT TO MOLD YOU INTO AN EVEN BETTER VERSION OF YOURSELF. THIS LIFE IS CRAZY. IT'S FUCKED UP AT TIMES. BUT IT IS MADE JUST FOR YOU. LIVE IT AND TAKE CARE OF YOURSELF.

www.ingramcontent.com/pod-product-compliance
Lightning Source LLC
Chambersburg PA
CBHW021121020426
42331CB00004B/574